iZZi English

Alphabet

Workbook+Tracing Letters

*English is easy
with iZZi English*

Written by Inga Terlizzi
Cover design by Anna Komendant

Some images and icons in this book are adapted from Freepik.com and Iconscount.com (premium licenses). Additional licensed images are sourced from Dreamstime.com, and all visuals have been customized for educational purposes.

Written by Inga Terlizzi
Cover design by Anna Komendant

ISBN: 979-8-9987564-2-9 (paperback)

Visit the author's website at www.izzienglish.org

For further information, please contact:
ingaterlizzi@izzienglish.org

Printed in the United States of America

Hi! My name is Miss English,
but you can call me iZZi

Welcome to **iZZi Alphabet,** my friend!
Let's learn the **ABCs** together —
with joy, curiosity, and lots of fun!

What's your name?

_____

Alphabet

There are 26 letters in the English Alphabet

Aa Bb Cc Dd

Ee Ff Gg Hh

Ii Jj Kk Ll Mm

Nn Oo Pp Qq

Rr Ss Tt Uu Vv

Ww Xx Yy Zz

4

Find the Pair
Draw lines to match the letters

A	l	**N**	p
B	c	**O**	u
C	a	**P**	q
D	j	**Q**	n
E	k	**R**	x
F	h	**S**	t
G	b	**T**	s
H	d	**U**	w
I	i	**V**	v
J	e	**W**	z
K	g	**X**	y
L	m	**Y**	o
M	f	**Z**	r

5

Read Aloud!
Alphabet Flashcards

Apple

A a

Ball

B b

Cat

C c

Dog

D d

Egg

E e

Fox

F f

Girl

G g

Hat

H h

Ice

I i

Read and Match
Draw lines to match the pictures

- Apple
- Ball
- Cat
- Dog
- Egg
- Fox
- Girl
- Hat
- Ice

Read Aloud!
Alphabet flashcards

Jam

Jj

Key

Kk

Lion

Ll

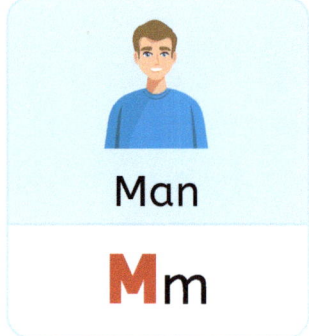

Man

Mm

Nest

Nn

Ox

Oo

Pineapple

Pp

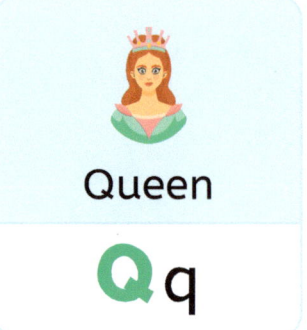

Queen

Qq

Rat

Rr

Read and Match
Draw lines to match the pictures

- **J**am

- **K**ey

- **L**ion

- **M**an

- **N**est

- **O**x

- **P**ineapple

- **Q**ueen

- **R**at

Read Aloud!
Alphabet flashcards

Sun

S s

Toy

T t

Umbrella

U u

Van

V v

Wig

W w

Xylophone

X x

Yogurt

Y y

Zebra

Z z

Read and Match
Draw lines to match the pictures

- **S**un

- **T**oy

- **U**mbrella

- **V**an

- **W**ig

- **X**ylophone

- **Y**ogurt

- **Z**ebra

Alphabet (A–M)
Tracing capital letters

A — A A A A

B — B B B B

C — C C C C

D — D D D D

E — E E E E

F — F F F F

G — G G G G

H — H H H H

I — I I I I

J — J J J J

K — K K K K

L — L L L L

M — M M M M

Alphabet (N-Z)
Tracing capital letters

N N N N N

O O O O O

P P P P P

Q Q Q Q Q

R R R R R

S S S S S

T T T T T

U U U U U

V V V V V

W W W W W

X X X X X

Y Y Y Y Y

Z Z Z Z Z

Alphabet (a-m)
Tracing small letters

a a a a a

b b b b b

c c c c c

d d d d d

e e e e e

f f f f f

g g g g g

h h h h h

i i i i i

j j j j j

k k k k k

l l l l l

m m m m m

Alphabet (n-z)
Tracing small letters

n   n n n n

o   o o o o

p   p p p p

q   q q q q

r   r r r r

s   s s s s

t   t t t t

u   u u u u

v   v v v v

w   w w w w

x   x x x x

y   y y y y

z   z z z z

Alphabet Order

Fill in the missing alphabet letters in the empty bubbles

One is Different
Find the odd letter in each row

C

1   A   B   ~~C~~   D   E   F

2   E   F   G   H   I   L

3   I   J   K   L   W   N

4   K   L   M   N   Q   P

5   R   C   T   U   V   W

6   U   V   M   X   Y   Z

Little Letters Party!
Write the *small* letter

A a

B __

C __

D __

E __

F __

G __

H __

I __

J __

K __

L __

M __

N __

O __

P __

Q __

R __

S __

T __

U __

V __

W __

X __

Y __

Z __

Big Letters Parade!
Write the *capital* letter

A	a		j		s
	b		k		t
	c		l		u
	d		m		v
	e		n		w
	f		o		x
	g		p		y
	h		q		z
	i		r		

Find the Pair

Draw lines to match *the capital letter* with *the small letter*

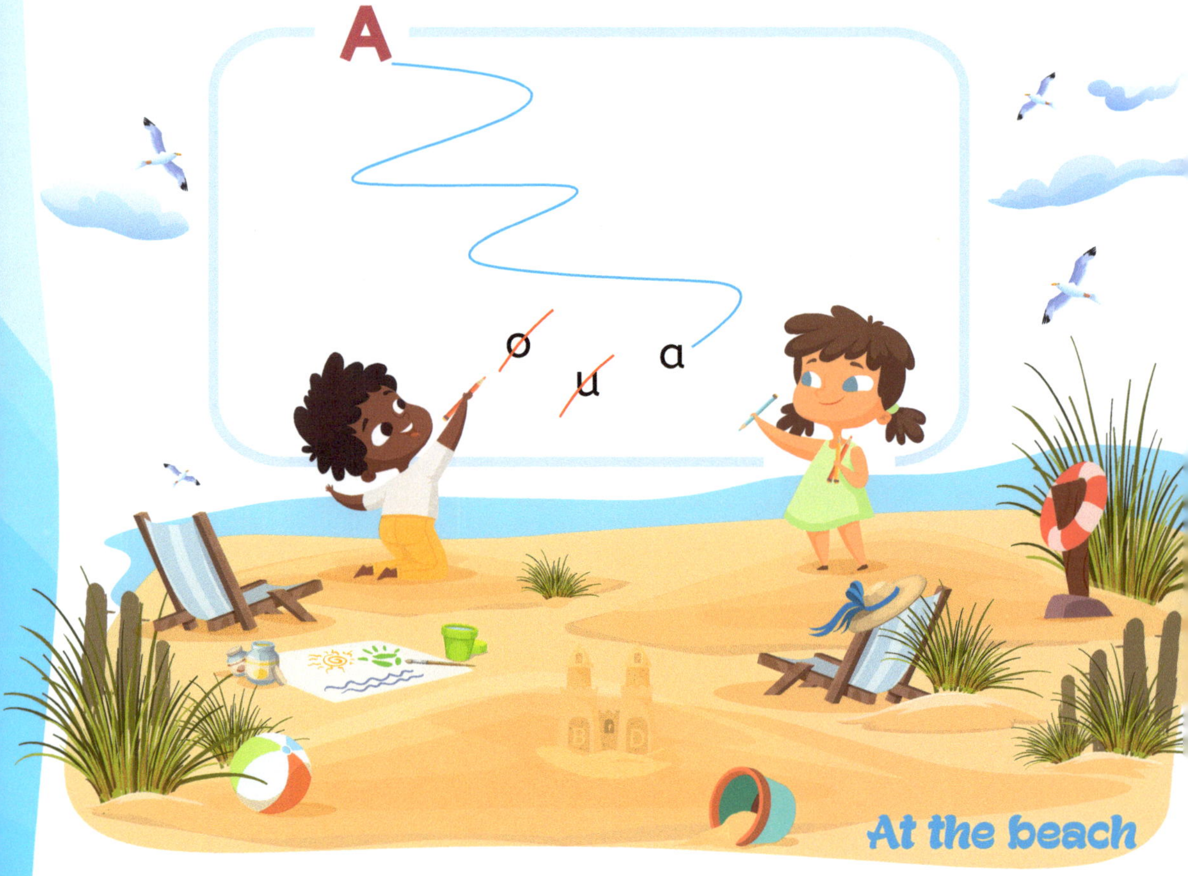

A
o
u
a
At the beach

A			B		
a	o	u	d	p	b

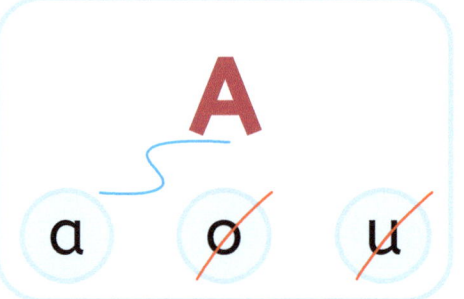

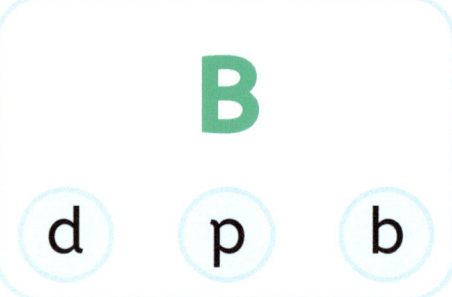

Inspired by the New Jersey shore

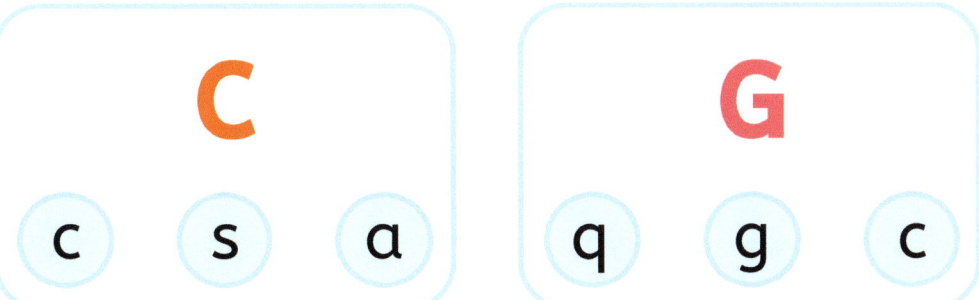

C — c   s   a

G — q   g   c

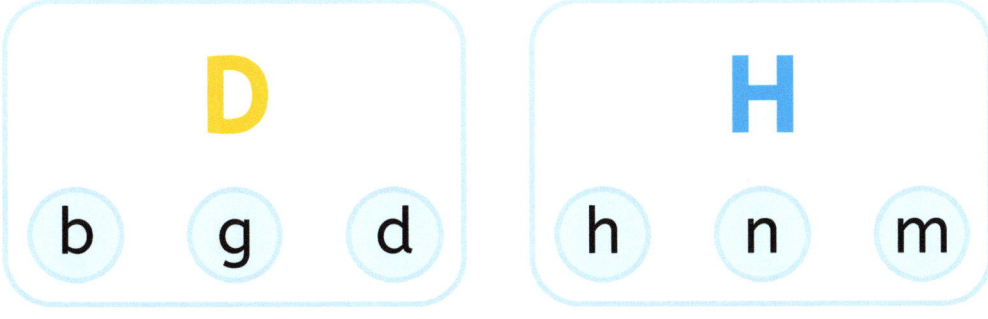

D — b   g   d

H — h   n   m

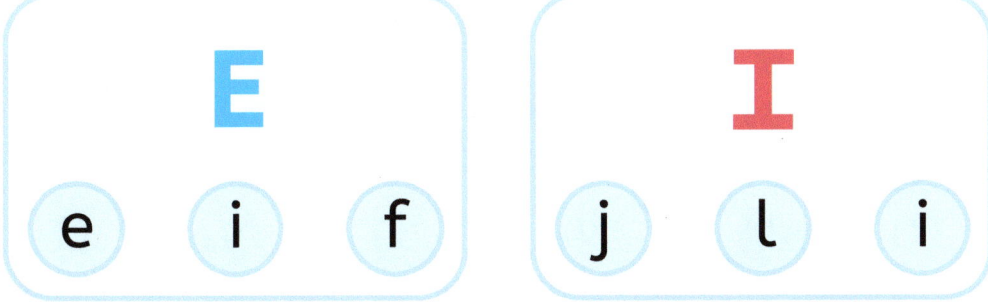

E — e   i   f

I — j   l   i

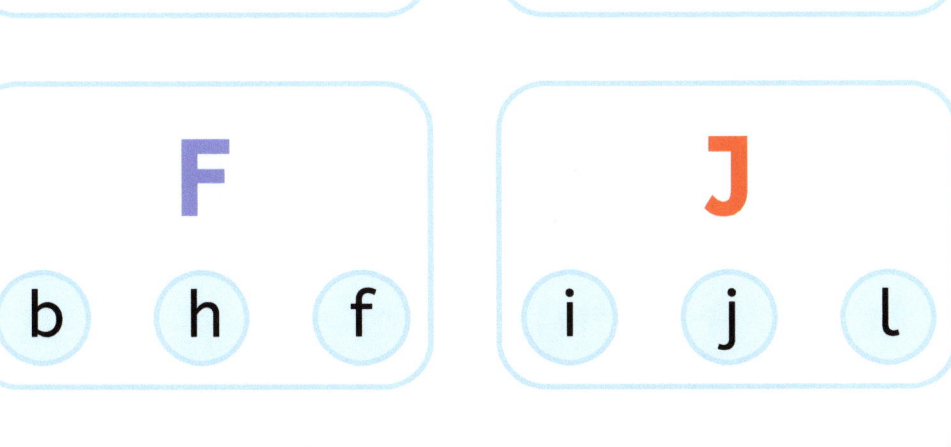

F — b   h   f

J — i   j   l

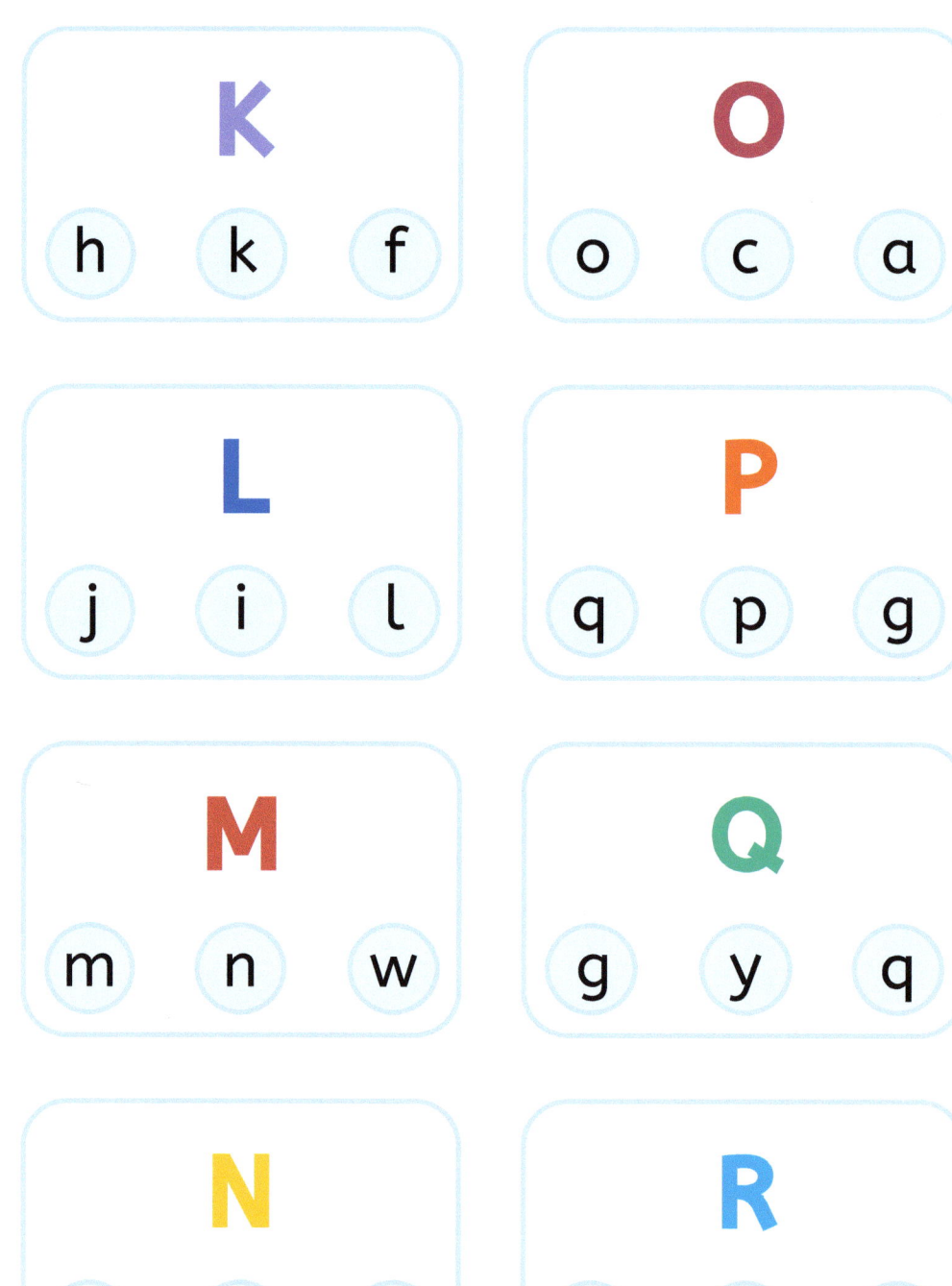

K
h k f

O
o c a

L
j i l

P
q p g

M
m n w

Q
g y q

N
u n m

R
r p n

S

c o s

W

w m v

T

k t l

X

z s x

U

u n v

Y

u y v

V

v u y

Z

r s z

Look Closely!

Find and circle
all the same
letters in the box

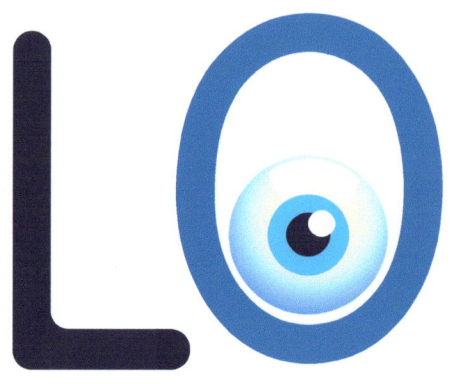

a, b, d, p

a

p	(a)	q	a	b
a	q	b	a	q
q	a	q	q	a

b

p	b	p	b	b
b	p	b	b	p
p	b	p	p	b

d

q	d	q	d	d
d	q	q	q	d
q	d	d	d	q

p

p	b	b	q	p
b	p	p	q	b
q	b	p	b	q

**Glasses clear,
letters near!**

P, O, M, X

		P		
R	P	P	B	P
P	B	R	P	R
P	R	P	B	P

		O		
O	Q	D	O	C
O	O	Q	O	D
D	C	O	O	C

		M		
M	N	W	M	W
M	M	N	M	N
W	M	M	N	W

		X		
K	X	K	X	Y
Y	K	X	Y	X
X	Y	X	K	X

25

ABC Detective

Write the letters in alphabetical
order in each group

a - m

a b c d e f g h i j k l m

1 c e a ———————— a c e

2 d h b ———————— ☐ ☐ ☐

3 i f k ———————— ☐ ☐ ☐

4 g j m ———————— ☐ ☐ ☐

n - z

n o p q r s t u v w x y z

1 r p n ———————— ☐ ☐ ☐

2 q o t ———————— ☐ ☐ ☐

3 u s m ———————— ☐ ☐ ☐

4 z x v ———————— ☐ ☐ ☐

Letter Neighbors

Write the letter that comes before and after each letter below

Q R S

_____ E _____

_____ M _____

_____ X _____

_____ B _____

_____ O _____

_____ S _____

_____ D _____

_____ T _____

_____ G _____

_____ U _____

A   N
B   O
C   P
D   Q
E   R
F   S
G   T
H   U
I   V
J   W
K   X
L   Y
M   Z

_____ C _____

_____ F _____

_____ V _____

_____ L _____

_____ K _____

_____ F _____

_____ V _____

_____ H _____

_____ N _____

_____ J _____

_____ I _____

27

Wake-Up, Alphabet

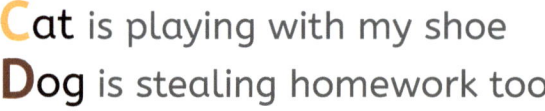

Alarm is ringing by my head
Breakfast smells — I jump from bed

Cat is playing with my shoe
Dog is stealing homework too

Eggs are flying from the pan
Fruits are jumping on the floor

Glasses hiding from the man
Hats are hanging on the door

Ice is swimming in my juice
Jam is gone — the jar is loose

Keys are hiding in my coat
Lion's napping in my boat

Mom is calling, "We are late"
Nose gets bumped — I close the gate

Orange slips into my bag
Pen draws faces, blue and red

Quiz at school begins too fast
Rain is falling hard and fast

Shoes are wet, I slip and fall
Teacher watches from the hall

Umbrella flies into the sky
Van drives past, and splashes high

Window shuts upon my hand
Xylophone plays a funny song

Yogurt drips into the stream
Zebra laughs — it's just a dream!

29

Find the First Letter
Look at the picture and fill in the first letter

1   A l a r m

2  ☐ r e a k f a s t

3  ☐ a t

4  ☐ i o n

5  ☐ g g s

6 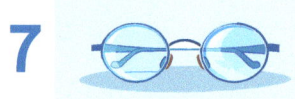 ☐ a m

7 ☐ l a s s e s

30 *Check the words on Page 28*

Find the First Letter
Look at the picture and fill in the first letter

1  ☐ r a n g e

2  ☐ a i n

3  ☐ e n

4  ☐ h o e s

5  ☐ m b r e l l a

6  ☐ a n

7  ☐ e b r a

Check the words on Page 29

31

Dot to Dot

Draw the otter by connecting
the letters in order